HUMAN RESOURCE MANAGEMENT

STRATEGIES FOR BUILDING AND MANAGING A HIGH-PERFORMANCE TEAM

DR. JAGADEESH PILLAI

Made with ♥ on the Notion Press Platform
www.notionpress.com

|| Dedicated to all wisdom seekers around the world ||

ഇ

Contents

Contents

PRAYER

"Om Bhadram Karnebhih Shrunuyaama DevaahBhadram Pashyemaakshabhiryajatraah SthirairangaistushtuvaamsastanoobhihVyashema Devahitam YadaayuhSwasti Na Indro VridhashravaahSwasti Nah Pooshaa VishwavedaahSwasti Nastaarkshyo ArishtanemihSwasti No Brihaspatir DadhaatuOm Shantih, Shantih, Shantih"

The literal meaning of this mantra is: OM. O Gods! Let us hear auspicious words from our ears. O reverent Gods! Let us behold propitious visions from our eyes, let our organs and body be stable, healthy, and strong. Let us do that which is pleasing to the gods in the life span allotted to us. May Indra, inscribed in the scriptures, bring us fortune! May Pushan, the knower of the world, grant us prosperity! May Trakshya, who vanquishes enemies, bestow us with blessings! May Brihaspati bring us success!
OM Peace, Peace, Peace.

ABOUT THE AUTHOR

Dr. Jagadeesh Pillai is a renowned Guinness World Record holder, writer, and researcher hailing from Varanasi, also known as the abode of Lord Shiva. With a Ph.D. in Vedic Science and a range of creative ideas and achievements, he is a true polymath. He is the author of more than 100 books including Research Publications. Although his roots can be traced back to Kerala, the people of Varanasi hold him in high regard and affectionately consider him one of their own.

In 1998, Dr. Pillai was offered a job at Banaras Hindu University, but he left the position after only two months to pursue greater goals in life. He believed that in order to study Indian scriptures and engage in other creative endeavours, he needed to retire from the daily grind of working solely for money at a young age.

He started an export business from scratch, using the knowledge he had gained from a previous job in the industry. His intelligence and unique approach to business led to great success in a short period of time, earning him more in just a decade and a half than he would have in a lifetime working in a government job. Upon the passing of Dr. APJ Abdul Kalam, Dr. Pillai decided to leave the business and dedicate himself to reading, studying, researching, and experimenting.

During his tenure in the export business, Dr. Pillai traveled to over 16 countries, gaining valuable insight and experiencing the world and life in detail.

Dr. Pillai has achieved four Guinness World Records in the following subjects:

"Script to Screen" - In this record, Dr. Pillai produced and directed an animation film within the shortest time possible, breaking the previous record set by Canadians. He has also received numerous national and international awards and recognitions for this achievement.

Longest Line of Postcards - For this record, Dr. Pillai created a line of 16,300 postcards on the occasion of the 163rd anniversary of Indian Postal Day. The event also included a questionnaire about the Indian flag.

Largest Poster Awareness Campaign - Dr. Pillai designed an awareness campaign on the subject of "Beti Bachao - Beti Padhao" (Save the Girl Child - Educate the Girl Child) to achieve this record.

Largest Envelope - In tribute to the Indian Prime Minister's "Make in India" initiative, Dr. Pillai created a 4000 square meter envelope using waste paper to achieve this record.

Attempted - **70000 Candles on a 210 kg Cake** - To celebrate the 70th Indian Independence Day, Dr. Pillai attempted to light 70,000 candles on a 210 kg cake, which was recorded in World Records India.

Attempted - **Documentary on Dhamek Stupa of Sarnath in 17 Languages** - Dr. Pillai attempted to create a documentary on the Dhamek Stupa of Sarnath, dubbing it in 17 different languages. The result of this attempt is currently awaiting confirmation from the Guinness World Records.

Dr. Pillai is skilled in teaching the Bhagavad Gita, a Hindu scripture, and is popular among young people. He has helped many young people improve their lives through his motivational teachings.

In addition to teaching, he has composed and sung numerous Sanskrit Bhajans and patriotic songs.

He has also written and directed several short films and documentaries for awareness campaigns, and has volunteered with the police in both UP and Kerala to spread awareness about various issues through videos and photography.

Incredibly, he has produced and directed over 100 documentaries about the city of Varanasi, all on his own.

He has also helped and guided more than 25 boys and girls to achieve world records through creative and innovative methods. He is a multifaceted person who uses his intellect and the blessings given to him by God to excel in various areas. He is both a teacher and a student, always learning and teaching, and is able to master any subject he comes across.

He is a selfless social activist and motivational speaker who has overcome struggles and failures to become a successful and enthusiastic individual with a rich life experience.

In addition to his work with the Bhagavad Gita, he is also an efficient Tarot card reader, Astro-Vastu consultant, and a talented singer and composer. He has sung the entire Ram Charita Manas and Bhagavad Gita in his own compositions, and has sung the phrase "Lokah Samastha Sukhino Bhavantu" in 50 different languages. He is currently working on a detailed and scientific study of Vedas, Upanishads, Puranas, and the Bhagavad Gita. He has also composed and sung the Hanuman Chalisa and Gayatri Mantra in 108 and 1008 different compositions, respectively.

Awards - Four Times Guinness World Records, Winner of Mahatma Gandhi Vishwa Shanti Puraskar, Mahatma Gandhi Global Peace Ambassador, Kashi Ratna Award, Dr. APJ Abdul Kalam Motivational Person of the Year 2017, Mother Teresa Award, Indira Gandhi Priyadarshini Award, Bharat Vikas Ratna Award, Udyog Ratna Award, Vigyan Prasar Award, Poorvanchal Ratn Samman.

PREFACE

Human resource management is a critical function of any organization, as it is responsible for attracting, developing, and retaining the best talent to drive business success. In today's rapidly changing business environment, it is more important than ever for organizations to have effective HR strategies in place to build and manage high-performance teams.This book, "Human Resource Management: Strategies for Building and Managing a High-Performance Team," is designed to provide readers with a comprehensive understanding of the key principles and practices of HR management. It covers a wide range of topics, including recruitment and selection, employee development, performance management, compensation and benefits, and workplace safety and security.

In addition to providing an overview of key HR concepts and practices, the book also includes practical strategies and tools that organizations can use to build and manage high-performance teams. Whether you are a HR professional, a manager, or a business leader, this book will provide you with the knowledge and skills you need to effectively manage your organization's most valuable asset – its people.

The book is written by experts in the field of HR management and includes real-world examples and case studies to illustrate key concepts and provide context. It is designed to be a valuable resource for anyone looking to understand and improve their organization's HR practices.

We hope that this book will serve as a valuable guide for building and managing high-performance teams, and that it will provide you with the knowledge and tools you need to achieve success in your organization.

I

Introduction to Human Resource Management

Human Resource Management (HRM) is the process of acquiring, developing, and maintaining a skilled workforce for an organization. It involves a wide range of activities, including recruiting and hiring, training and development, performance management, compensation and benefits, and compliance with labor laws and regulations. The ultimate goal of HRM is to create a high-performance team that can effectively support the organization's mission, vision, and strategic goals.

In this chapter, we will provide an overview of the key concepts and principles of HRM. We will explore the role of HRM in an organization, the different functions and responsibilities of HR professionals, and the challenges and opportunities facing HRM today. We will also discuss the importance of building and managing a high-performance team, and the strategies and best practices that can be used to achieve this goal.

The Role of HRM in an Organization

HRM plays a vital role in the success of an organization. It is responsible for attracting, developing, and retaining a talented and motivated workforce that can support the organization's mission and vision. Additionally, HRM plays a key role in creating a positive and productive work environment, managing employee relations, and ensuring compliance with labor laws and regulations.

The Functions and Responsibilities of HR Professionals

HR professionals are responsible for a wide range of tasks and activities, including recruiting and hiring, training and development, performance management, compensation and benefits, and compliance with labor laws and regulations. They also play a key role in creating a positive and productive work environment and managing employee relations.

Challenges and Opportunities Facing HRM Today

HRM is facing a number of challenges and opportunities in today's rapidly changing business environment. Some of the key challenges include:

Attracting and retaining top talent

Managing a diverse and global workforce

Keeping up with new technologies and changes in the workforce

Managing employee engagement and productivity

Ensuring compliance with labor laws and regulations

Some of the key opportunities for HRM include:

Leveraging new technologies to improve HR processes and performance

Developing and implementing effective strategies for managing a diverse and global workforce

Building and managing a high-performance team

Enhancing employee engagement and productivity

Building and Managing a High-Performance Team

Building and managing a high-performance team is essential for the success of an organization. A high-performance team is one that is motivated, engaged, and committed to achieving the organization's mission and vision. To build and manage a high-performance team, HR professionals can use a variety of strategies and best practices, including:

Recruiting and hiring the right people

Providing training and development opportunities

Building a positive and productive work environment

Managing employee relations and engagement

Implementing effective performance management systems

In conclusion, HRM plays a vital role in the success of an organization and is responsible for attracting, developing, and retaining a talented and motivated workforce. In this chapter, we have provided an overview of the key concepts and principles of HRM, including the role of HRM in an organization, the different functions and responsibilities of HR professionals, and the challenges and opportunities facing HRM today. We have also discussed the importance of building and managing a high-performance team and the strategies and best practices that can be used to achieve this goal.

II

Talent Acquisition and Recruitment

Talent acquisition and recruitment are essential functions of Human Resource Management (HRM) that involve identifying, attracting, and hiring the right people to fill the organization's workforce needs. The process of talent acquisition and recruitment is crucial for building and maintaining a high-performance team, as it enables organizations to attract and retain top talent that can support the organization's mission, vision, and strategic goals.

The recruitment process typically begins with identifying the workforce needs of the organization. This includes determining the number of employees needed, the qualifications and skills required, and the job duties and responsibilities. Once the workforce needs have been identified, the organization can begin the process of attracting and recruiting candidates.

One of the key strategies for attracting and recruiting candidates is to create a strong employer brand. Employer branding is the process of developing and communicating an organization's reputation as a desirable place to work. This can be done by highlighting the organization's culture, values, and benefits, as well as by providing information about the organization's mission, vision, and strategic goals.

Another strategy for attracting and recruiting candidates is to use a variety of recruitment methods, such as online job postings, employee referrals, and recruitment agencies. Online job postings are a popular method for reaching a large number of potential candidates, while employee referrals can provide valuable insights into the qualifications and skills of potential candidates. Recruitment agencies can also help organizations identify and attract candidates with the right qualifications and skills.

Once potential candidates have been identified, the organization can begin the process of screening and selecting the best candidates for the job. This typically involves conducting interviews, background checks, and reference checks. The organization should also take into account any legal requirements and regulations related to the recruitment process.

Finally, once the best candidates have been selected, the organization can make job offers and onboard the new hires. Onboarding is the process of introducing new employees to the organization and familiarizing them with the company culture, policies, and procedures. It is an essential step in the recruitment process that helps new hires become productive and engaged members of the organization.

In conclusion, talent acquisition and recruitment are essential functions of HRM that involve identifying, attracting, and hiring the right people to fill the organization's workforce needs. The process of talent acquisition and recruitment is crucial for building and maintaining a high-performance team and it involves creating a strong employer brand, using a variety of recruitment methods, conducting interviews, background checks, and reference checks. Additionally, onboarding is an essential step that helps new hires become productive and engaged members of the organization.

III

Employee Onboarding and Orientation

Employee onboarding and orientation are critical components of the Human Resource Management (HRM) process that help to integrate new employees into the organization and ensure that they are equipped with the knowledge, skills, and resources needed to be successful in their new roles.

Onboarding typically begins before an employee's first day on the job and continues for several weeks or months after the employee starts working. The goal of onboarding is to provide new employees with a positive and smooth transition into the organization and to help them feel welcomed and valued.

The onboarding process typically includes several key

elements such as:

Pre-boarding: This involves preparing for the new employee's arrival by setting up their workstation, providing necessary equipment and technology, and ensuring that they have access to the appropriate resources and information.

Orientation: This involves providing new employees with an overview of the organization, its culture, values, policies, and procedures. This is typically done through a formal orientation program that includes presentations, tours, and meetings with key personnel.

Training: This involves providing new employees with the skills, knowledge, and tools they need to perform their job effectively. This may include job-specific training, as well as training on company policies, procedures, and systems.

Mentoring and coaching: This involves pairing new employees with experienced mentors or coaches who can provide guidance, support, and feedback to help them adjust to their new roles.

Integration and socialization: This involves helping new employees to integrate into the organization by providing opportunities to meet and interact with colleagues, and by involving them in team-building activities and social events.

Onboarding and orientation are not just a one-time event, but a continuous process that should be reviewed, evaluated and improved regularly to ensure that it meets the needs of the organization and the new employees.

In conclusion, employee onboarding and orientation are critical components of the HRM process that help to integrate new employees into the organization and ensure that they are equipped with the knowledge, skills, and resources needed to be successful in their new roles. This process includes pre-boarding, orientation, training, mentoring and coaching, and integration and socialization. These steps are meant to ensure a smooth transition and positive experience for the new employee and to increase their engagement, retention and productivity.

IV

Employee Training and Development

Employee training and development are important functions of Human Resource Management (HRM) that aim to enhance the knowledge, skills, and abilities of employees to improve their performance and support the organization's goals.

Training is the process of providing employees with the knowledge and skills they need to perform their current job effectively. This can include job-specific training, as well as training on company policies, procedures, and systems. Training can be provided in various forms such as classroom-based instruction, on-the-job training, e-learning, or self-paced learning.

Development, on the other hand, is the process of preparing employees for future roles or responsibilities within the organization. This can include skills development, leadership development, and career advancement opportunities. Development programs can be in the form of mentoring, coaching, job rotations, and tuition reimbursement.

Effective employee training and development can lead to a number of benefits for the organization, such as:

Increased productivity: By providing employees with the knowledge and skills they need to perform their job effectively, organizations can improve productivity and efficiency.

Improved quality: Training and development can also help organizations improve the quality of their products and services by providing employees with the skills and knowledge they need to identify and address quality issues.

Increased employee engagement and retention: Employees who feel that their skills and knowledge are being developed are more likely to be engaged and satisfied with their job, which can lead to increased retention.

Increased adaptability: Training and development can also help organizations to adapt to changes in the business environment by providing employees with the skills and knowledge they need to respond to new challenges and opportunities.

Improved bottom-line results: By investing in employee training and development, organizations can improve their bottom-line results by increasing productivity, improving quality, and reducing employee turnover.

In conclusion, employee training and development are important functions of HRM that aim to enhance the knowledge, skills, and abilities of employees to improve their performance and support the organization's goals. Training is the process of providing employees with the knowledge and skills they need to perform their current job effectively, while development is the process of preparing employees for future roles or responsibilities within the organization. Effective employee training and development can lead to increased productivity, improved quality, increased employee engagement and retention, increased adaptability, and improved bottom-line results.

V

Performance Management

Performance management is a process used by organizations to evaluate and improve the performance of their employees. It is an ongoing process that involves setting performance expectations, providing feedback and coaching, and measuring and evaluating performance.

The process typically includes several key elements such as:

Setting performance expectations: This involves clearly defining the goals and objectives that employees are expected to achieve, as well as the standards of performance that are expected.

Providing feedback and coaching: This involves regularly providing employees with feedback on their performance, as well as coaching and support to help them improve.

Measuring and evaluating performance: This involves using various methods to measure and evaluate employee performance, such as performance appraisals, 360-degree feedback, and self-evaluations.

Providing rewards and recognition: This involves recognizing and rewarding employees who have met or exceeded performance expectations.

Identifying and addressing performance issues: This involves identifying and addressing any performance issues that may arise, such as poor performance or underperformance, and taking appropriate action to correct them.

Performance management is a continuous process that should be reviewed, evaluated, and improved regularly to ensure that it meets the needs of the organization and the employees.

Effective performance management can lead to a number of benefits for the organization, such as:

Improved productivity: By setting clear performance expectations and providing regular feedback, organizations can improve the productivity of their employees.

Increased employee engagement and motivation: By recognizing and rewarding employees who meet or exceed performance expectations, organizations can increase employee engagement and motivation.

Improved communication: Performance management can

also improve communication between employees and managers by providing regular opportunities for feedback and coaching.

Improved bottom-line results: Effective performance management can lead to improved bottom-line results by increasing productivity and reducing employee turnover.

In conclusion, performance management is a process used by organizations to evaluate and improve the performance of their employees. It is an ongoing process that involves setting performance expectations, providing feedback and coaching, measuring and evaluating performance, providing rewards and recognition, and identifying and addressing performance issues. Performance management should be reviewed, evaluated, and improved regularly to ensure that it meets the needs of the organization and the employees. Effective performance management can lead to improved productivity, increased employee engagement and motivation, improved communication, and improved bottom-line results.

VI

Compensation and Benefits

Compensation and Benefits

Compensation and benefits are important functions of Human Resource Management (HRM) that aim to attract, retain, and motivate employees.

Compensation refers to the total amount of money and benefits that an employee receives in exchange for their work. It includes base pay, bonuses, and other forms of financial compensation such as stock options or profit-sharing.

Benefits are non-monetary forms of compensation that include things like health insurance, retirement plans, vacation time, and other perks.

Compensation and benefits play an important role in

attracting and retaining employees. Organizations that offer competitive compensation and benefits packages are more likely to attract and retain talented employees. Additionally, an effective compensation and benefits program can help increase employee satisfaction, motivation, and productivity.

An effective compensation and benefits program should:

Be competitive: Organizations should ensure that their compensation and benefits packages are competitive with those offered by other organizations in the same industry.

Be fair: Organizations should ensure that their compensation and benefits packages are fair and equitable for all employees.

Be flexible: Organizations should offer a range of compensation and benefits options that can be tailored to meet the individual needs of employees.

Be easy to understand: Organizations should ensure that their compensation and benefits packages are easy for employees to understand and access.

Be reviewed and updated regularly: Organizations should review and update their compensation and benefits packages regularly to ensure they are still competitive, fair, and meet the changing needs of employees.

In conclusion, compensation and benefits are important functions of HRM that aim to attract, retain, and motivate employees. Compensation refers to the total amount of money and benefits that an employee receives in exchange for their work, while benefits are non-monetary forms of compensation that include things like health insurance, retirement plans, vacation time, and other perks. An effective compensation and benefits program should be competitive, fair, flexible, easy to understand, and reviewed and updated regularly.

VII

Employee Engagement and Retention

Employee engagement and retention are closely related aspects of Human Resource Management (HRM) that focus on creating a positive and productive work environment that encourages employees to stay with the organization.

Employee engagement refers to the level of involvement, enthusiasm, and commitment that employees have towards their work and the organization. Engaged employees are more likely to be productive, motivated, and committed to the organization's goals and objectives.

Retention, on the other hand, refers to the ability of an organization to keep its employees over time. High employee turnover can be costly for an organization in terms of recruitment, training, and lost productivity.

Effective strategies for employee engagement and retention include:

Clear communication: Encourage open and transparent communication between employees and management. This helps employees feel informed and included in the organization's decision-making process.

Recognition and rewards: Acknowledge and reward employees for their contributions to the organization. This helps to increase employee engagement and motivation.

Professional development opportunities: Provide employees with opportunities for professional development and growth. This helps employees to feel challenged and valued.

Flexibility: Offer flexible work arrangements such as telecommuting or flexible hours, as this can help employees balance their work and personal lives.

Employee involvement: Involve employees in the decision-making process and in the design of their work. This helps employees to feel valued and invested in their work.

Employee well-being: Create a positive work environment that promotes employee well-being, this can include things like mental health support, time off, etc.

In conclusion, employee engagement and retention are closely related aspects of HRM that focus on creating a positive and productive work environment that encourages employees to stay with the organization. Effective strategies for employee engagement and retention include clear communication, recognition and rewards, professional development opportunities, flexibility, employee involvement, and employee well-being. By implementing these strategies, organizations can help increase employee engagement, motivation, and retention, which can lead to improved productivity and bottom-line results.

VIII

Employee Relations and Communication

Employee relations and communication are important functions of Human Resource Management (HRM) that aim to foster a positive and productive work environment by promoting effective communication and healthy relationships between employees and management.

Employee relations refers to the ongoing interactions and relationships between employees and management. It includes activities such as labor-management negotiations, employee grievances and complaints, and union-management relations. Effective employee relations help to foster a positive and productive work environment by promoting trust, cooperation, and mutual understanding between employees and management.

Communication, on the other hand, refers to the exchange of information and ideas between employees and management. Effective communication helps to ensure that employees are informed about the organization's goals, policies, and procedures, and that their concerns and suggestions are heard and considered.

Effective strategies for employee relations and communication include:

Clear and transparent communication: Encourage open and transparent communication between employees and management. This helps employees feel informed and included in the organization's decision-making process.

Employee involvement: Involve employees in the decision-making process and in the design of their work. This helps employees to feel valued and invested in their work.

Regular feedback: Provide employees with regular feedback on their performance, and encourage them to give feedback to management. This helps to build trust and mutual understanding.

Employee representation: Encourage employee representation on committees and in other decision-making bodies. This helps to promote cooperation and collaboration between employees and management.

Conflict resolution: Develop effective conflict resolution procedures to help resolve disputes between employees and management.

Employee engagement: Encourage employee engagement by creating opportunities for employees to share their ideas, suggestions and concerns.

In conclusion, employee relations and communication are important functions of HRM that aim to foster a positive and productive work environment by promoting effective communication and healthy relationships between employees and management. Effective strategies for employee relations and communication include clear and transparent communication, employee involvement, regular feedback, employee representation, conflict resolution and employee engagement. By implementing these strategies, organizations can help build trust, cooperation, and mutual understanding between employees and management, which can lead to improved productivity, employee satisfaction and retention.

IX

Employee Health and Wellness

Employee health and wellness is an important aspect of Human Resource Management (HRM) that focuses on promoting and maintaining the physical, mental and emotional well-being of employees. A healthy and well-informed workforce is more productive, less absent and has a better performance.

Effective strategies for employee health and wellness include:

Promote healthy habits: Encourage employees to adopt healthy habits such as regular exercise, healthy eating, and stress management.

Provide wellness programs: Offer wellness programs such as fitness classes, health screenings, and health education.

Mental health support: Provide mental health support for employees, such as counseling and employee assistance programs.

Encourage work-life balance: Encourage employees to maintain a balance between their work and personal lives.

Provide a safe and healthy work environment: Create a safe and healthy work environment by providing proper training, equipment, and resources to promote employee well-being.

Flexible working arrangements: Offer flexible working arrangements such as telecommuting or flexible hours.

Employee Assistance Programs: Provide Employee Assistance Programs (EAP) which are designed to provide employees with confidential counseling and support services to help them manage personal and work-related issues.

In conclusion, employee health and wellness is an important aspect of HRM that focuses on promoting and maintaining the physical, mental and emotional well-being of employees. Effective strategies for employee health and wellness include promoting healthy habits, providing wellness programs, mental health support, encouraging work-life balance, providing a safe and healthy work environment, flexible working arrangements and Employee Assistance Programs. By implementing these strategies, organizations can help improve employee well-being, which can lead to improved productivity, employee satisfaction, and retention.

X

Diversity, Equity, and Inclusion

Diversity, equity, and inclusion (DEI) are important aspects of Human Resource Management (HRM) that focus on creating a workplace environment that is inclusive and respectful of all individuals, regardless of their race, ethnicity, gender, sexual orientation, religion, age, and ability. DEI initiatives aim to create a culture of respect and understanding, where everyone feels valued and included, and where everyone can reach their full potential.

Effective strategies for DEI include:

Develop a DEI strategy: Develop a comprehensive DEI strategy that outlines the organization's commitment to diversity, equity, and inclusion, and sets specific goals and targets.

Increase diversity in the workforce: Increase diversity in the workforce by recruiting and hiring from underrepresented groups, and by providing training and development opportunities.

Promote equity: Promote equity by providing fair and equal opportunities for all employees, regardless of their background.

Foster an inclusive culture: Foster an inclusive culture by encouraging open communication, providing training on cultural competency, and promoting a culture of respect and understanding.

Provide resources for underrepresented groups: Provide resources, such as employee resource groups, for underrepresented groups to support their professional development and to promote a sense of belonging.

Regularly monitor and measure progress: Regularly monitor and measure progress on DEI goals, and make adjustments as necessary to ensure that the organization is meeting its commitments.

Hold leadership accountable: Hold leadership accountable for creating a culture of DEI, by promoting a culture of respect, equity, and inclusion throughout the organization.

In conclusion, Diversity, equity, and inclusion (DEI) are important aspects of Human Resource Management (HRM) that focus on creating a workplace environment that is inclusive and respectful of all individuals, regardless of their race, ethnicity, gender, sexual orientation, religion, age, and ability. Effective strategies for DEI include developing a DEI strategy, increasing diversity in the workforce, promoting equity, fostering an inclusive culture, providing resources for underrepresented groups, regularly monitoring and measuring progress, and holding leadership accountable. By implementing these strategies, organizations can create a culture of respect, equity, and inclusion, which can lead to improved productivity, employee satisfaction, and retention.

XI

Talent Management

Talent management is an important aspect of Human Resource Management (HRM) that focuses on identifying, developing, and retaining the most talented and capable employees within an organization. Talent management involves a range of activities, including talent acquisition, employee development, and succession planning.

Effective strategies for talent management include:

Identify key talents: Identify key talents within the organization and provide them with development opportunities to help them reach their full potential.

Create a career development plan: Create a career development plan for each employee, which outlines the steps they need to take to achieve their career goals.

Provide training and development opportunities: Provide training and development opportunities to help employees improve their skills and knowledge.

Succession planning: Develop a succession plan to ensure that key positions within the organization are filled by capable and qualified employees, in the event of a vacancy.

Employee engagement: Encourage employee engagement by providing opportunities for employees to provide feedback and to have a voice in decision-making processes.

Performance management: Use performance management to identify and reward high-performing employees, and to provide guidance and support for under-performing employees.

Retention strategies: Implement retention strategies to keep high-performing employees within the organization, such as competitive compensation and benefits packages, flexible working arrangements, and a positive work-life balance.

In conclusion, Talent management is an important aspect of Human Resource Management (HRM) that focuses on identifying, developing, and retaining the most talented and capable employees within an organization. Effective strategies for talent management include identifying key talents, creating a career development plan, providing training and development opportunities, succession planning, employee engagement, performance management, and retention strategies. By implementing these strategies, organizations can attract, develop and retain talented employees, which can lead to improved productivity, employee satisfaction, and long-term success.

XII

Succession Planning

Succession planning is an important aspect of Human Resource Management (HRM) that focuses on identifying and developing employees to fill key leadership roles within an organization. The goal of succession planning is to ensure that the organization has a pipeline of qualified and capable individuals who are ready to step into leadership roles when they become available.

Effective strategies for succession planning include:

Identify key positions: Identify key positions within the organization that are critical to the success of the business and that would be difficult to fill if a vacancy occurred.

Identify potential successors: Identify potential successors for key positions by assessing the skills, experience, and potential of current employees.

Develop a talent pipeline: Develop a talent pipeline by providing development opportunities, such as training, mentoring, and job rotations, to employees identified as potential successors.

Create a career development plan: Create a career development plan for each potential successor, outlining the steps they need to take to reach their goals and prepare for a leadership role.

Provide ongoing support and guidance: Provide ongoing support and guidance to potential successors, including coaching and mentoring, to help them develop the skills and knowledge they need to succeed in a leadership role.

Regularly review and update the plan: Regularly review and update the succession plan to ensure that it is aligned with the organization's goals and that potential successors are on track to reach their goals.

Communicate the plan: Communicate the succession plan to key stakeholders within the organization, including employees, managers, and the board of directors, to ensure that everyone is aware of the plan and its goals.

In conclusion, Succession planning is an important aspect of Human Resource Management (HRM) that focuses on identifying and developing employees to fill key leadership roles within an organization. Effective strategies for succession planning include identifying key positions, identifying potential successors, developing a talent pipeline, creating a career development plan, providing ongoing support and guidance, regularly reviewing and updating the plan and communicating the plan. By implementing these strategies, organizations can ensure that they have a pipeline of qualified and capable individuals ready to step into leadership roles when they become available, which can lead to improved productivity, employee satisfaction, and long-term success.

XIII

Organizational Culture

Organizational culture refers to the shared values, beliefs, norms, and practices that shape the way people think, feel, and behave within an organization. It is the personality of the organization and sets the tone for how employees interact with one another, as well as with customers and other stakeholders.

Effective strategies for managing organizational culture include:

Clearly define and communicate the organization's values and mission: Clearly define and communicate the organization's values and mission to all employees, so that they understand the company's purpose and direction.

Lead by example: Lead by example, and model the behavior that the organization wishes to promote.

Encourage open communication: Encourage open communication among employees, and provide opportunities for them to share their ideas, thoughts, and feedback.

Foster a positive work environment: Foster a positive work environment by recognizing and rewarding employees for their contributions, and by creating opportunities for them to connect with one another.

Invest in employee development: Invest in employee development by providing training and development opportunities that promote the organization's values and culture.

Celebrate successes: Celebrate successes, both big and small, to reinforce the organization's culture and foster a sense of pride among employees.

Be adaptable: Be adaptable to change, and be open to feedback and suggestions on how to improve the organizational culture.

In conclusion, Organizational culture refers to the shared values, beliefs, norms, and practices that shape the way people think, feel, and behave within an organization. Effective strategies for managing organizational culture include clearly defining and communicating the organization's values and mission, leading by example, encouraging open communication, fostering a positive work environment, investing in employee development, celebrating successes, and being adaptable to change. By fostering a positive and supportive organizational culture, organizations can improve employee satisfaction, productivity, and engagement, which can lead to long-term success.

XIV

Human Resource Information Systems (HRIS)

Human Resource Information Systems (HRIS) are computerized systems that are used to manage and automate human resource processes and functions. These systems can be used to track and manage employee information, such as personal data, payroll, benefits, and performance evaluations. They can also be used to automate other HR processes, such as recruitment, onboarding, and training.

Effective strategies for implementing and utilizing an HRIS include:

Define the business needs: Define the business needs and goals of the organization, and determine how an HRIS can support those needs.

Research and select an appropriate system: Research and select an appropriate system that meets the organization's needs and budget.

Develop a plan for implementation: Develop a plan for implementing the system, including timelines, budget, and resources.

Train employees: Train employees on how to use the system, and provide ongoing support to ensure its effective use.

Integrate with other systems: Integrate the HRIS with other systems, such as payroll and benefits, to ensure that data is accurate and up-to-date.

Regularly review and evaluate the system: Regularly review and evaluate the system to ensure it is meeting the organization's needs, and make changes as necessary.

Keep data secure: Keep data secure by implementing appropriate access controls and data backup procedures.

In conclusion, Human Resource Information Systems (HRIS) are computerized systems that are used to manage and automate human resource processes and functions. Effective strategies for implementing and utilizing an HRIS include defining the business needs, researching and selecting an appropriate system, developing a plan for implementation, training employees, integrating with other systems, regularly reviewing and evaluating the system, and keeping data secure. An effective HRIS can save time and effort by automating HR processes, improve data accuracy and security, and increase the efficiency of HR processes and decision making.

XV

Employee Law and Regulations

Employee law and regulations refer to the laws and regulations that govern the employment relationship, including issues such as wages, hours, discrimination, safety, and benefits. These laws and regulations are put in place to protect the rights of employees and to ensure fair and equitable treatment in the workplace.

Effective strategies for managing employee law and regulations include:

Stay informed: Stay informed about the latest laws and regulations that may impact the organization and its employees, such as changes to minimum wage laws or new anti-discrimination laws.

Develop and implement policies and procedures: Develop and implement policies and procedures that comply with laws and regulations and that promote fair and equitable treatment of employees.

Provide training: Provide training to employees and managers on laws and regulations, including discrimination and harassment laws, wage and hour laws, and safety regulations.

Investigate and respond to complaints: Investigate and respond to complaints of potential violations of laws and regulations, and take appropriate action to address any issues that are identified.

Monitor compliance: Monitor compliance with laws and regulations, and conduct regular audits to ensure that the organization is in compliance.

Seek legal advice: Seek legal advice if there are any doubts about the organization's compliance with laws and regulations, or if there is a legal dispute with an employee or government agency.

Keep accurate records: Keep accurate records of compliance with laws and regulations, such as employee files, payroll records, and safety records.

In conclusion, Employee law and regulations refer to the laws and regulations that govern the employment relationship, which protect the rights of employees and ensure fair and equitable treatment in the workplace. Effective strategies for managing employee law and regulations include staying informed, developing and implementing policies and procedures, providing training, investigating and responding to complaints, monitoring compliance, seeking legal advice and keeping accurate records. By understanding and complying with employee laws and regulations, organizations can reduce the risk of legal disputes and ensure a fair and equitable workplace for all employees.

XVI
International Human Resource Management

International Human Resource Management (IHRM) refers to the process of managing the human resources of an organization that operates in multiple countries. This includes recruiting, hiring, training, and managing employees in different cultural and legal environments. IHRM also includes managing the cultural and legal differences that may impact the employment relationship.

Effective strategies for managing international human resource management include:

Understand cultural differences: Understand the cultural differences that may impact the employment relationship, such as differences in communication styles, work ethics, and management practices.

Develop a global recruitment strategy: Develop a global recruitment strategy that takes into account the different cultural and legal requirements of different countries.

Provide cross-cultural training: Provide cross-cultural training to employees to help them understand and adapt to different cultural and legal environments.

Implement effective communication: Implement effective communication strategies to ensure that all employees are informed and engaged, regardless of their location.

Establish policies and procedures: Establish policies and procedures that comply with the laws and regulations of each country in which the organization operates.

Manage expatriate employees: Manage expatriate employees effectively by providing them with support, such as language training and cultural orientation.

Use technology: Use technology to communicate, collaborate and share information with employees in different countries.

In conclusion, International Human Resource Management (IHRM) refers to the process of managing the human resources of an organization that operates in multiple countries. Effective strategies for managing IHRM include understanding cultural differences, developing a global recruitment strategy, providing cross-cultural training, implementing effective communication, establishing policies and procedures that comply with the laws and regulations of each country in which the organization operates, managing expatriate employees and using technology to communicate and share information with employees in different countries. By managing IHRM effectively, organizations can recruit, train and manage employees in different cultural and legal environments, while minimizing the cultural and legal differences that may impact the employment relationship.

XVII

Human Resource Planning

Human Resource Planning (HRP) is the process of forecasting an organization's future workforce needs and determining how to meet those needs. This includes identifying the number and types of employees that will be needed, as well as the skills and qualifications required to perform the work. HRP also includes developing strategies to attract and retain the necessary workforce, as well as managing the impact of workforce changes on the organization.

Effective strategies for Human Resource Planning include:

Conduct a workforce analysis: Conduct a workforce analysis to determine the current and future workforce needs of the organization, including the number and types of employees that will be needed, as well as the skills and qualifications required to perform the work.

Develop a recruitment and retention plan: Develop a recruitment and retention plan to attract and retain the necessary workforce, including strategies for recruiting and retaining employees with the necessary skills and qualifications.

Implement an employee development plan: Implement an employee development plan to ensure that employees have the skills and knowledge needed to perform their jobs effectively, including training and development programs.

Manage workforce transitions: Manage workforce transitions, such as retirements and layoffs, by identifying and developing replacement employees, and by providing support to affected employees.

Use technology: Use technology, such as human resource information systems (HRIS) to analyze workforce data, forecast workforce needs, and track employee performance and development.

Monitor and evaluate HRP: Monitor and evaluate HRP by tracking key performance indicators (KPIs) such as employee turnover, recruitment costs, and the cost of employee development.

In conclusion, Human Resource Planning (HRP) is the process of forecasting an organization's future workforce needs and determining how to meet those needs. Effective strategies for Human Resource Planning include conducting a workforce analysis, developing a recruitment and retention plan, implementing an employee development plan, managing workforce transitions, using technology, and monitoring and evaluating HRP. By planning effectively for the organization's workforce needs, organizations can ensure that they have the right number and types of employees, with the necessary skills and qualifications, to achieve their business goals.

XVIII

Change Management

Change management is the process of planning, implementing, and managing changes in an organization. This includes changes to the organization's structure, processes, systems, and culture. Change management is important because it helps organizations adapt to new circumstances and achieve their goals.

Effective strategies for change management include:

Develop a change management plan: Develop a change management plan that outlines the steps that will be taken to implement the change, including timelines, resources, and key stakeholders.

Communicate effectively: Communicate effectively with all stakeholders, including employees, customers, and partners, to ensure that they understand the reasons for the change, the benefits, and the impact on their roles and responsibilities.

Prepare employees for the change: Prepare employees for the change by providing training and development opportunities, as well as support for the transition.

Involve employees in the change process: Involve employees in the change process by involving them in the design and implementation of the change. This helps to build support for the change and to identify potential issues.

Monitor and evaluate the change: Monitor and evaluate the change by tracking key performance indicators (KPIs) such as employee engagement, customer satisfaction, and business performance.

Continuously improve: Continuously improve the change management process by learning from experience, and by making adjustments as needed.

Foster a culture of change: Foster a culture of change by encouraging employees to embrace new ideas, to think differently and to be open to new ways of doing things.

In conclusion, Change management is the process of planning, implementing, and managing changes in an organization. Effective strategies for change management include developing a change management plan, communicating effectively, preparing employees for the change, involving employees in the change process, monitoring and evaluating the change, continuously improving, and fostering a culture of change. By managing change effectively, organizations can achieve their goals, and adapt to new circumstances. This is key for the success and long-term sustainability of the organization.

XIX

Workplace Safety and Security

Ensuring the safety and security of employees is a critical responsibility for any organization. A safe and secure work environment not only protects employees from harm, but it also promotes productivity and reduces employee turnover. The following strategies can help organizations create a safe and secure work environment.

Develop a safety and security plan: Organizations should develop a comprehensive safety and security plan that outlines procedures for responding to emergencies, such as natural disasters, fires, and active shooter situations. The plan should also include guidelines for identifying and reporting potential safety hazards, as well as procedures for investigating and correcting hazards.

Train employees on safety and security procedures: Employees should be trained on the organization's safety and security procedures, including emergency evacuation procedures and how to report potential hazards. Additionally, employees should be trained on how to respond to emergency situations, such as active shooter situations.

Conduct regular safety and security audits: Organizations should conduct regular safety and security audits to identify potential hazards and ensure that safety and security procedures are being followed. These audits should be conducted by trained professionals and should include a review of the organization's safety and security plan, as well as a physical inspection of the work environment.

Implement security measures: Organizations should implement security measures to protect employees and assets from theft and other forms of crime. These measures may include security cameras, security guards, and access control systems.

Encourage employee participation: Employees should be encouraged to participate in the organization's safety and security efforts. This can include reporting potential hazards, participating in safety and security training, and serving on safety and security committees.

Communicate safety and security policies clearly: Safety and security policies should be communicated clearly to all employees, and should be easily accessible.

By implementing these strategies, organizations can create a safe and secure work environment that protects employees and promotes productivity.

XX
Employee Privacy

Protecting the privacy of employees is an important responsibility for any organization. Employee privacy laws vary by jurisdiction, but generally, employers are required to protect the personal information of their employees, such as their name, address, and Social Security number. Additionally, employers have a responsibility to protect the privacy of employee medical information, financial information, and other sensitive data. The following strategies can help organizations protect employee privacy.

Develop a privacy policy: Organizations should develop a comprehensive privacy policy that outlines the types of information that will be collected and how it will be used, stored, and protected. The policy should also include guidelines for obtaining employee consent for the collection and use of personal information.

Train employees on privacy procedures: Employees should be trained on the organization's privacy procedures, including how to handle sensitive information and how to report suspected privacy violations.

Implement security measures: Organizations should implement appropriate security measures to protect employee personal information from unauthorized access, use, and disclosure. These measures may include firewalls, encryption, and access controls.

Conduct regular privacy audits: Organizations should conduct regular privacy audits to identify potential privacy risks and ensure that privacy procedures are being followed. These audits should be conducted by trained professionals and should include a review of the organization's privacy policy and procedures, as well as a physical inspection of the work environment.

Limit access to sensitive information: Access to sensitive employee information should be limited to only those employees who have a need to know.

Communicate privacy policies clearly: Privacy policies should be communicated clearly to all employees, and should be easily accessible.

By implementing these strategies, organizations can protect the privacy of their employees and comply with legal requirements.

XXI

Human Resource Metrics and Analytics

Measuring and analyzing human resource (HR) data is essential for understanding the effectiveness of HR strategies and making data-driven decisions. By collecting and analyzing data on key HR metrics such as employee turnover, engagement, and performance, organizations can identify areas for improvement, track progress over time, and measure the return on investment of HR initiatives. The following strategies can help organizations effectively use HR metrics and analytics.

Identify key metrics: Organizations should identify key metrics that are relevant to their specific HR strategies and goals. These may include metrics such as employee turnover, engagement, and performance.

Collect data: Organizations should establish systems for collecting data on key HR metrics. This may include surveys, interviews, and other forms of data collection. Data should be collected regularly and consistently.

Analyze data: Organizations should analyze collected data to identify trends, patterns, and areas for improvement. This may include creating reports and dashboards, conducting statistical analyses, and identifying correlations and causations.

Communicate findings: Organizations should communicate the findings of their data analysis to relevant stakeholders, such as HR managers, executives, and employees. This may include creating visualizations, reports, and presentations.

Take action: Organizations should use the insights gained from their data analysis to make data-driven decisions and take action to improve HR strategies and outcomes. This may include making changes to recruitment and retention strategies, developing employee development programs, and implementing new HR technologies.

Continuously monitor: Organizations should continuously monitor their HR metrics and make adjustments as needed to ensure that they are achieving their desired outcomes.

By implementing these strategies, organizations can effectively use HR metrics and analytics to improve their human resource management and achieve their desired outcomes.

XXII

Labor Relations

Labor relations refer to the interactions between an organization and its employees, including issues related to wages, hours, and working conditions. Organizations have a responsibility to treat their employees fairly and in accordance with labor laws and regulations. The following strategies can help organizations effectively manage labor relations.

Develop policies and procedures: Organizations should develop clear policies and procedures for dealing with issues related to wages, hours, and working conditions. These policies should be communicated clearly to all employees, and should be in compliance with all relevant labor laws and regulations.

Maintain open communication: Organizations should maintain open communication with employees and their representatives to address any concerns or issues related to labor relations. This may include regular meetings with employee representatives, such as union representatives or employee councils.

Negotiate with employee representatives: Organizations should negotiate with employee representatives on issues related to wages, hours, and working conditions. This may include collective bargaining agreements with unions or other forms of negotiation with employee councils or other representatives.

Mediate disputes: Organizations should have procedures in place to mediate disputes between employees and management. This may include using internal or external mediators, or utilizing other forms of dispute resolution.

Comply with labor laws and regulations: Organizations should comply with all relevant labor laws and regulations, including those related to wages, hours, and working conditions. This may include complying with minimum wage laws, overtime laws, and safety regulations.

Organizations should continuously monitor their labor relations and make adjustments as needed to ensure that they are treating their employees fairly and in compliance with all relevant laws and regulations.

By implementing these strategies, organizations can effectively manage labor relations, treat employees fairly, and comply with all relevant laws and regulations.

XXIII

Human Resource Outsourcing

Human resource outsourcing (HRO) is the practice of hiring an external company to handle certain HR functions, such as recruitment, payroll, and benefits administration. Outsourcing can help organizations save time and money, while also allowing them to focus on their core business operations. The following strategies can help organizations effectively outsource HR functions.

Identify functions to outsource: Organizations should identify which HR functions they wish to outsource. This may include recruitment, payroll, benefits administration, and other functions.

Conduct a vendor search: Organizations should conduct a thorough vendor search to find a reputable and experienced HRO provider. This may include researching potential vendors, conducting interviews, and obtaining references.

Negotiate a contract: Organizations should negotiate a contract with the chosen HRO provider, outlining the specific services that will be provided, the terms of the agreement, and the pricing structure.

Implement the service: Organizations should implement the outsourcing service, including transferring data and providing training to employees on how to use the new service.

Continuously monitor: Organizations should continuously monitor the outsourcing service to ensure that it is meeting their needs and providing value. This may include regularly reviewing performance metrics, conducting satisfaction surveys, and conducting regular reviews of the service.

Continuously evaluate the partnership: Organizations should continuously evaluate the partnership to ensure that it aligns with their business objectives and that they are getting the expected outcome.

By implementing these strategies, organizations can effectively outsource HR functions and improve their overall HR operations.

XXIV

Human Resource Consulting

Human resource consulting is the practice of providing expert advice and support to organizations on various HR-related issues, such as recruitment, employee relations, and compliance. Consulting services can help organizations improve their HR practices and achieve their desired outcomes. The following strategies can help organizations effectively use HR consulting services.

Identify areas for improvement: Organizations should identify specific areas of their HR practices where they need improvement. This may include recruitment, employee relations, or compliance with labor laws and regulations.

Conduct a consultant search: Organizations should conduct a thorough search to find a reputable and experienced HR consultant. This may include researching potential consultants, conducting interviews, and obtaining references.

Establish clear objectives: Organizations should establish clear objectives for the consulting engagement, including desired outcomes, timelines, and budget.

Implement the consulting services: Organizations should implement the consulting services, including providing the consultant with necessary information and data and following their recommendations.

Continuously monitor: Organizations should continuously monitor the consulting engagement to ensure that it is meeting their needs and providing value. This may include regularly reviewing performance metrics, conducting satisfaction surveys, and conducting regular reviews of the service.

Continuously evaluate the partnership: Organizations should continuously evaluate the partnership with the consultant to ensure that it aligns with their business objectives and that they are getting the expected outcome.

By implementing these strategies, organizations can effectively use HR consulting services to improve their HR practices and achieve their desired outcomes.

XXV
Human Resource Auditing

Government and non-profit organizations have unique operational challenges, as they often have limited resources and must comply with specific regulations. The following strategies can help these organizations effectively manage their operations.

Understand regulations and compliance requirements: Government and non-profit organizations must comply with specific regulations, such as those related to procurement, data privacy, and financial reporting. It is important for organizations to understand these requirements and ensure that their operations are in compliance.

Optimize resource allocation: Government and non-profit organizations often have limited resources, and it is important for them to optimize resource allocation to ensure that they are using resources efficiently and effectively. This may include using data and analytics to identify areas of inefficiency and implementing cost-saving measures.

Develop partnerships: Government and non-profit organizations can benefit from developing partnerships with other organizations, such as other government agencies, non-profits, and private sector companies. These partnerships can provide access to additional resources and expertise, and can help organizations achieve their goals more effectively.

Foster a culture of transparency and accountability: Government and non-profit organizations must be transparent and accountable to the public, stakeholders, and funders. It is important for these organizations to foster a culture of transparency and accountability, and to communicate regularly with stakeholders about their operations and performance.

Continuously monitor and evaluate: Government and non-profit organizations should continuously monitor and evaluate their operations to ensure that they are achieving their goals and using resources effectively. This may include conducting regular reviews, implementing performance metrics, and soliciting feedback from stakeholders.

By implementing these strategies, government and non-profit organizations can effectively manage their operations, comply with regulations, and optimize resource allocation to achieve their goals.

Other Books Of The Author

1. The Moments When I Met God
2. Kashiyile Theertha Pathangal
3. GURU GYAN VANI
4. Abhiprerak Gita
5. ASSI SE JAIN GHAT TAK
6. Hopelessness of Arjuna
7. The Soul and It's True Nature
8. Sense of Action (Karma)
9. Action through Wisdom
10. Action through Wisdom
11. THEORY AND PRACTICAL OF EVERY ACTION
12. LOGICAL UNDERSTANDING OF THE SUPREME
13. THE IMPERISHABLE SUPREME
14. Yatra Nishadraj se Hanuman Ghat Tak
15. Yatra Karnatak Ghat se Raja Ghat Tak
16. Yatra Pandey Ghat se Prayagraj Ghat Tak
17. Yatra Ranjendra Prasad Ghat se Dattatreya Ghat Tak
18. YaatraSindhiya Ghat se Gwaliar Ghat Tak
19. Yatra Mangala Gauri Ghat se Hanuman Gadhi Ghat Tak
20. Yatra Gaay Ghat Se Nishad Ghat Tak
21. MAA GANGA, GHATEN EVM UTSAV
22. Ganga Arti Dev Deepavali evam Any Utsav
23. Potentials of Digitalized India
24. VEDIC CONSCIOUSNESS
25. A Brief Introduction to Vedic Science
26. Kashi ke Barah Jyotirling
27. IMPACT OF MOTIVATION
28. Let's have a Milky Way Journey
29. Color Therapy in a Nutshell

30. Rigveda in a Nutshell
31. Yajurveda in a Nutshell
32. Samveda in a Nutshell
33. Atharva Veda in a Nutshell
34. Ayushman Bhava - Ayurveda
35. Srimad Bhagavad Gita and Upanishad Connection
36. Srimad Bhagavad Gita - an attempt to summarize each chapter.
37. Facts and Impact of Nakshatra
38. Astro Gems - NAVARATNA
39. Ekadashi - A Concise Overview
40. A Concise View of Hanuman Chalisa
41. Inspirational Gita
42. Nakshatraranyam
43. Summary of 18 Mahapuranas
44. Synopsis of 18 Upa Puranas
45. Rigvediya Upanishads
46. Shukla Yajurvediya Upanishads
47. Krishna Yajurvediya Upanishads
48. Samavediya Upanishads
49. Atharvavediya Upanishads
50. The Seven Great Sages
51. From Rocket Scientist to President Dr. APJ Abdul Kalam
52. The Visionary's Voice - Quotes of Dr. APJ Abdul Kalam
53. The Wisdom of Swami Vivekananda: Insights and Inspiration from a Legendary Spiritual Teacher
54. Ayurvedic Remedies from the Garden
55. Sages and Seers
56. Rising Strong – Motivational Stories of Women
57. Beyond Flames -Mystery stories of Funeral Ghat Manikarnika
58. The Origins of Tulsi: A Look at the Mythological Roots of the Plant"

59. The Holistic Cow: A Look at the Physical, Spiritual, and Cultural Importance of Cows in India
60. Arts of Healing
61. Exploring the Divine
62. Understanding Five Elements
63. The Etymology of Ram
64. Symbols of India
65. Voice of Change (About Speeches of Great Men)
66. She Speaks (About Speeches of Great Women)
67. Patriotism on Celluloid – Brief About Patriotic Films
68. The Music of Motivation: A Brief Guide to Inspirational Film Songs
69. **Unlocking the Secrets of the Dashopanishads**
70. A Cultural Mosaic
71. Ancient Traditions, Modern Minds
72. Ecos of Ancient Wisdom
73. Beneath the Surface
74. From Temples to Ashrams
75. Sages of the Subcontinent
76. The Art of Healling (Ayurveda, Yoga & Naturopathy)
77. Indian Kitchen
78. The Festivals of India
79. The Indian Epics Retold
80. The Power of Mantras
81. The Indian River Ganges
82. The Indian Architecture
83. Rites of Passage
84. The Indian Silk Road
85. The Indian Literature
86. The Indian Villages
87. The Indian Folks & Crafts
88. The Way of Buddha
89. The Ramayan of Tulsidas

90. Astrological Remedies
91. The Secret Power of Motivation
92. Secret of Developing your Inner Strength
93. The Secret Path to Motivation
94. The Art and Secret of Positive Thinking
95. The Secrets of Practicing Ethical Living
96. Indian Art and Painting
97. The Indian Herbalism
98. Bharatanatyam to Kathak
99. Exploring India's Astrological Remedies
100. The Indian Festival of Flowers
101. Indian Handicrafts
102. The Splashes of Joy – India's Colour Festival
103. The Indian Science of Astrology
104. The Indian Mythology
105. Path to Enlightenment
106. The Indian Spirituality for Children
107. Aromas of India
108. The Secrets of Healthy Relationships
109. Ancestral Ties
110. The Indian Street Food
111. Discovering America
112. The Indian Textile
113. Listening to Motivational Speeches
114. Taste of India
115. A Cultural Journey through Indian Nuptials
116. Motivational Quote for Change
117. Secret Strategies for Making Money
118. Secrets to Cultivate a Positive Mindset
119. A Tapestry of Cultures: Exploring India from Kashmir to Kanyakumari
120. Achieving Your Dreams with Resilience: Secret Strategies for Overcoming Obstacles

121. Innovative Startups - 25 Startup Ideas to Spark Your Business Creativity
122. Export Management: Strategies for Global Success
123. Exporting from India - A Step by Step Guide
124. Finance Fundamentals: Mastering Financial Management for Business Success
125. Global Growth Strategies for International Business Development
126. Marketing Mastery: Unlocking the Secrets of Modern Marketing
127. Operations Mastery: Managing the Flow of Value in Business
128. Strategic Business Management: Navigating the Modern Business Landscape
129. Human Resource Management Strategies for Building and Managing a High Performance Team

CONTACT

DR. JAGADEESH PILLAI

MBA & PhD in Vedic Science

Four Times Guinness World Record Holder

Winner of Mahatma Gandhi Vishwa Shanti Puraskar and Global Peace Ambassador

Gemology, Astro & Vastu Consultant - Spiritual Counselor

Consultant for designing World Record Ideas

Efficient Tarot Card Reader

9839093003

myrichindia@gmail.com

drjagadeeshpillai@facebook

drjagadeeshpillai@instagram
jagadeeshpillai@youtube

www. JAGADEESHPILLAI.com

|| LOKAHA SAMASTHAHA SUKHINO BHAVANTU ||

Printed by Libri Plureos GmbH in Hamburg, Germany